My Soul Exposed

By Zahra Naderi

This book of poetry is dedicated to my beautiful parents,
Belquess and Sadi Naderi. They breathe strength into my soul
and give me life every day.

Contents

Introduction

Dear Readers,

I thank you for the interest you have shown to enter my world of poetry and to read my prose. This book has been a dream of mine for longer than I can remember; a dream to write, to express and to touch people's lives through the power of words. Writing is a powerful form of expression; it is a beautiful yet dangerous tool if not used sensitively and I dedicate this book to all those in search of life's great answers. In search of purpose and truth. Divided into 3 sections; Soul, Self and Love, this short collection of my most personal poems explores the multiple facets that form our identity. I hope that my readers will connect to my words at the deepest level and feel its energy, for poetry is my soul language and this book my purpose.

Yours truly,
Zahra Naderi

Prologue

What is written
On your heart
That makes the
World sway
In your direction?
What flower blooms
In your soul
When you are
Aligned to your
Path in life?
What feelings
Do you get
When the universe
Applauds you
In your success?
Tell me
What echoes
In your soul
And what drives
Your goals?
For it is me
For it is I
Who guides you

In the direction
Of your dreams,
Dreams you have
Yet to explore.
My dear,
Knowing
Your truth
Is the reality of
Your Existence

My Soul Exposed

Welcome to
My world,
Roses and
Their thorns
With sunny
Rainy days

Soul

Let me
Wonder
At my soul,
Let me feel
Its intensity
As I sit here
Awakened
By a vibration
So healing
That I cannot even
Comprehend its
Power,
Yet I know
It exists.
My soul is
Alive
My spirit
Feels
My body
Elated

Empowered,
I am connected
To my soul
My higher self
My vision
My own
Personal muse,
A soul
Exploring
I vibrate so
Highly,
A frequency
So strong,
Let me feel its
Magnificence
Finally.
For I have waited
So long
To unveil
This spirit
To the
World

Pause
And listen,
It is amidst
Silence
Where you will
Find your
Answers,
I can only see
What the mind
Allows me to see,
Yet when I
Connect
With my soul
I feel a sense of
Knowing,
To separate
Real from fake
True from false
And to capture the
Light of
My Being

Can you
See me?
Do you know
Who I am?
My soul speaks
To you in ways
You cannot
Understand
Why do I feel
Such emptiness
From your side?
I thought I was
The gem
The golden spark
You've shattered
My world
My energy
My soul
Wow, I say
In awe of one
Charming stare
For it is done
You've finished
Your run

Keep going,
For it is
The soul
That guides you
Not the mind,
The mind is a
Slave to the
World,
The soul is
Your
Kingdom

Untangle
Yourself
From the
Chains of the
Material world,
I cry so deep
It hurts to
Breathe
For I am
Eternal,
Separate from
My shoes
And my dress

When the
Path
Is right,
The soul knows,
It breathes
A little
Slower
It loves
A little
Deeper

Self

I am golden
Like the sun,
I feel
The heat
Burning in
My soul
Like a flame
In my chest,
I am
Awakened
To the
Sound of
The Spirits,
To the
Height of
The Heavens,
To the light
Shining brightly
In the deep
Blue sky

I am more
Than a
Woman,
I am heart
I am soul
I am the cream
To my coffee,
The jam
To my scone
And I will
Continue to
Shine,
Sweet like
Honey
Fiery like
The Sun

To feel
What I feel
Is to become me,
To know the
Thoughts
That circulate
Within me
Is to
Understand
Me,
To look within
Thyself
Is to build
Empathy,
What can I do
To expand
Your spiritual
World?
It is no deception
We must grow
As one first,
To be one of
Eternity

Am I
Defined
By my roots?
My dark
Brown curls
My honey
Milk skin
My flag of
Many colours
Or that I
Am a woman?
My strength
Lies within me
And so does
My soul,
For it is that
Which
Defines me

We continue
To seek truth,
Yet the
Truth lies
Only within
Ourselves,
Look internally
For that is where
You will learn
Your worth

Continue to
Look deep
Within,
Only they who
Have truly felt,
Can understand
The true power
Of the spirit,
I say
Be free,
Live
And be
Born again

I sit with my
Thoughts,
Watching my
Breath,
Such heaviness
In my heart
And my legs
Like a sea of blue
It engulfs my senses
It has become me
Why do I feel such
Melancholy?
My heart,
My mind
And the physicals
Work well inside
Yet I feel in my spirit
A heaviness
I cannot comprehend
I seek to understand
Yet lacking in strength
I say I will continue
Continue to strive
But it is in these times
I seek council
From a higher power
To guide and lift me

For it cannot be
Done alone
I am tired.
I need air.
To breath.
To feel.
To live.
Must I awaken
Or perhaps
Shut down?
The battery is
Losing its power.
But let my
Enemy know,
This is only for
Now.

Covid-19

Love

My parents
Your strength,
Your soul,
Your weeping
Heart
Gifted to your
Body part
You feel so deep
With so much fire
I cannot compare
Your love
But only admire
The power
Of your essence
I feel deeply
In my heart
My breath,
My beat,
My life today
Is your hard work
I love you
Mother
I love you
Father
You are the air
To my lungs
The strength
To my bones
The essence
Of my soul

Looking into
The oceans
Of your eyes,
I began to seek
A love
That warmed
My soul,
With every breath
We took each
Passing day
I learned to love
The parts of me
That once refused
To heal
And with each
Smile
And laugh
And stealing glance
You brought
A peace
To my heart
Yet lit a fire within
I ask above
How blessed am I?
For it is in
Your Soul
I have found
My own

My love
Grew deep
It gained
Momentum,
He was
The one,
I knew from
Day,
His energy
Captivating
My heart,
His love now
Stapled to
My Chest

Forget the
Words
Not the
Feeling,
She
Echoed
In my
Heart

I hear
His voice,
A gentle
Whisper
To my ear
A lightness
To my heart
'You're on
The right path'
I hear him say,
I breathe
One sigh of relief
As I see his
Feathery coat
Drop beneath

I cannot
Escape you
Your body
Your soul
Your gaze
For I am golden
Laying in your sun
You drew me
Stars
You drew me
Flowers
You drew me
Life
But the midnight
Moon
Struck my heart
And I felt your
Claw
Within my soul
The sun has
Fallen
And I see no
Light
Darkness
Within me
No place to
Run

No place to
Hide
Am I alone
Again?
Left only with
My feathery guide
Floating
By my side

I love
To love,
Yet do I
Understand?
A word so simple
Yet so divine
What is this
Life we live?
Am I blinded
By the tales?
Let me scrape
Beneath the surface
Melt like ice cream
And escape
Into your
Cushiony arms,
You are
My love
My world
My spiritual
Realm

Your
Energy,
I love
The beauty
Of your heart
Resonating
Within me
As my soul
Comes to light
For I fell in love
With life
When I met
Your spirit
And you taught
Me
The real
Meaning of
True love

My Final Words

It is only in
Solitude
Where our
Soul
Begins
To speak,
Listen closely,
What do you
Hear?

Special Thanks

I wish to thank all the wonderful people in my life who have made this book come alive, you know who you are; my parents, my three brothers, my best friend and my close family and friends. Success is sweetest when celebrated with love.

About the Author

Zahra Naderi graduated from Barts and the London, School of Medicine and Dentistry in 2018 and is a full-time doctor living in London. 'My Soul Exposed' is her first published poetry collection and she hopes to continue writing prose alongside working as a medical doctor. She is a strong believer in promoting mental well-being and believes poetry is the purest form of expression that has the potential to encourage personal growth and healing. Outside of work and writing, Zahra loves to travel and spend time with her loved ones.

Printed in Great Britain
by Amazon

79857085R00031